STEWARDS NOT GATEKEEPERS

*How Great Leaders Build Trust, Develop
People, and Create Lasting Impact*

Thomas Wigington

Published by The Foundry Press

An imprint of QTR Foundry

Upper Marlboro, MD

QTRFoundry.com

Intellectual Property

Disclaimer

This book reflects the author's experiences and perspectives. It is intended for informational purposes only and does not constitute professional, legal, or financial advice. Readers are responsible for how they apply the material.

ISBN: 979-8-9956939-2-5

Cover and interior design by The Foundry Press

Table of Contents

Dedication

For the leaders who believed in me before I believed in myself,
and for those who taught me just as much by what they withheld
as by what they gave.

For the moments when guidance was clear,
and for the moments when it wasn't—
both shaped who I became.

And for those still becoming:
may you carry what you were given with intention,
and leave behind leadership that outlasts you.

Epigraph

Leadership is not what you are given—
it is what you choose to carry forward.

Introduction

A Letter to the Leader You Are Becoming

If you're reading this, you've probably felt it already.

You've heard seasoned leaders talk about *"this generation."* Sometimes it's said offhand. Sometimes it comes out sharp. Sometimes it lands like a caution sign. Even if no one has aimed it at you directly, you've felt what it does: it creates space—like the people coming up are a problem to manage instead of potential to grow.

This letter isn't here to defend you.
It's here to get you ready.

Because sooner than you expect, you'll be the leader someone else is reading. And what you take in now—quietly, almost without noticing—will shape the leader you become.

Leadership doesn't start with authority. It starts with your posture: the stories you tell yourself about other people's behavior, the way you speak about the people who frustrate you, the choices you make when the situation still feels unclear. Long before anyone hands you a title, you're deciding whether leadership is control or stewardship—blame or responsibility—ego or service.

Every generation walks into an organization already shaped by the one before it. You didn't build the systems you're entering, and you didn't write the norms you're expected to navigate. But you will live with the consequences—and eventually, you'll be responsible for what comes next.

Here's what most people don't tell emerging leaders early enough:
You're learning how to lead even when no one is teaching you.

You learn from what inspires you, and you learn from what disappoints you. You learn from leaders who invest in you—and, just as clearly, from the ones who don't. And if you're not paying attention, you'll start to pick up the very habits you once swore you'd never adopt: the language you cringed at, the assumptions you pushed back on, the shortcuts you promised you wouldn't take.

This book is meant to interrupt that drift.

It's not here to tell you you're right and everyone else is wrong. And it's not here to flatter your perspective or dismiss the experience of the people who came before you. What it offers is more useful than either: **awareness**—of how leadership culture gets passed down, how frustration turns into cynicism, and how good intentions can harden into habits.

One day you'll lead people younger than you. They'll see the world differently. They'll ask questions that catch you off guard and challenge assumptions you don't even remember learning. In those moments, you'll have a choice: repeat what you once heard, or become better than what you inherited.

Titles change. Roles shift. Authority moves on. What lasts is what you build in people—what you teach, what you model, how well you listen, and whether you prepare others to stand where you're standing now. That work doesn't begin at promotion. It begins the first time someone trusts you enough to watch how you move.

This book won't hand you all the answers. But it can help you ask better questions—about power, responsibility, and the kind of leader you want to be, even after your title changes.

You're not here to fix *this generation*.
You're here to **become the leader the next one deserves**.

Read slowly. Be honest with yourself. Decide early who you want to be—before the role starts making the decisions for you.

Leadership is already shaping you.

Now you will begin shaping it.

Who This Book Is For

This book is for leaders before they are fully recognized as leaders.

- The high performer others already rely on

- The new supervisor learning how to carry responsibility

- The team member noticing leadership gaps but not yet in control of them

- The leader navigating generational tension without losing trust

- The professional transitioning into environments where influence matters more than authority

If you have ever thought:

- "There has to be a better way to lead than this"

- "I don't want to become the leader I once struggled under"

- "I want to lead well before I'm given full authority"

Then you are exactly who this book was written for.

As you start Chapter 1, notice the first leadership moment that comes to mind.

BEFORE YOU BEGIN

This is not a test.

It is a starting point.

Capture what you think now—before this book begins to shape how you see leadership.

You do not need to answer everything perfectly.
You only need to answer honestly.

1. First Recognition

What parts of the introduction felt familiar to you?
(Think about moments, language, or behaviors you have already noticed.)

2. Early Signals

When you hear leaders talk about "this generation," what do you feel first?

☐ Defensive

☐ Motivated

☐ Dismissed

☐ Curious

☐ Unsure

☐ Indifferent

Why do you think that reaction shows up?

3. Leadership Models

Name one leadership behavior you want to carry forward— and one you do not.

Carry forward:

Leave behind:

4. Perspective Inventory

What experiences, skills, or viewpoints do you bring that may differ from those above you?
(Technology, communication, values, problem-solving, teamwork, etc.)

How might these differences become strengths instead of sources of friction?

5. Influence Without Authority

Where do people already listen to you or seek your input—even informally?

What kind of influence do you want to practice there?

6. Looking Ahead

Complete this sentence:

As I continue reading, I want to better understand how to...

Revisit This Page

Write today's date and return to this page after finishing the book.

Start date: _____
Revisit date: _____

Awareness is where leadership begins.

What you do with it is what defines you.

Author's Note

This is not a pause.
It is a starting line.

By the end, these questions won't land the same way.

PART I

BECOMING AWARE

Leadership does not begin with authority.
It begins with awareness.

What you are about to notice is not rare.

It is formative.

Before you are trusted with decisions, people, or direction, you are already being shaped by what you observe. You are learning how leadership works—often without realizing it—by absorbing language, habits, and assumptions from those around you, especially from those with power.

Part I is where we slow that process down.

Instead of rushing to fix leadership, you'll practice watching it: the phrases that create distance, the shortcuts that feel efficient, the moments when curiosity fades. Those signals matter because they form culture—and culture rarely changes just because someone gets a new title.

Awareness is not criticism.
It is preparation.

Along the way, you'll learn to spot:

- How language reveals leadership posture

- How labels replace understanding

- How shortcuts feel like wisdom before they feel like failure

These chapters are not here to make you cynical. They are here to make you **conscious**. Conscious of what you are learning, what you are normalizing, and what you may unknowingly carry forward.

Many leaders never pause at this stage. They advance with unexamined habits, only to confront them later when authority magnifies their impact. This book invites you to do the opposite—to choose awareness early, while it is still easy to adjust.

By the end of Part I, you should not feel confident.
You should feel **alert**.

Alert to the kind of leadership you admire.
Alert to the kind you reject.
Alert to the choices forming quietly beneath the surface.

Keep going.

Leadership is already teaching you.
Now you will learn how to listen.

Leadership in this book follows a progression.

You learn to see clearly before you act.
You learn to choose posture before you gain power.
You learn to contribute before you are recognized.
And ultimately, you learn to build leaders—not just outcomes.

2

Chapter 1

The First Time You Notice Bad Leadership

Most leaders can point to a moment like this, even if they can't pin down the date.

It's when you realize authority and leadership aren't the same thing.

Someone with rank, tenure, or influence says something that lands wrong. Not as a blowup. Not even as an argument. Just a phrase—casual, dismissive, or unexamined—that quietly creates distance.

That moment matters more than it looks like in real time.

In the introduction, you were asked to observe before you fix—to watch language, posture, and the quiet signals that shape culture long before titles appear.

This chapter begins at the moment that awareness usually becomes personal.

Early in your career, leadership rarely comes from programs or books first. It comes from proximity—watching how decisions are made, how frustration is expressed, and how people are discussed when they aren't in the room. Long before you're trusted with responsibility, you're absorbing models—good and bad—for how leadership works.

This is often where the phrase *"this generation"* appears for the first time.

It is rarely spoken with malice. More often, it is shorthand—an attempt to explain unfamiliar behavior, shifting norms, or a loss of control over outcomes that once felt predictable. But whatever the intent, the phrase carries weight. It draws a line between *us* and *them*. And once that line exists, development slows.

What you are noticing in that moment is not generational difference. You are noticing **distance**.

Distance shows up when leaders trade curiosity for categories—when complexity becomes labels and responsibility shifts downward. The discomfort you feel is not immaturity. It is awareness forming.

Most emerging leaders register this quietly. They don't challenge it. They file it away. Over time, one of two things often happens: cynicism starts to creep in, or the language begins to feel normal. Either way, it can shape you if you don't notice what it's doing.

This is the drift the introduction warned you about—the slow normalization of language and behavior you once questioned.

Cynicism can start to whisper that leadership is inherently flawed and not worth aspiring to. Normalization can start to whisper that this is simply "how leaders talk," and that adopting the same language is the price of belonging. Neither voice helps you become the kind of leader you respect.

One of the first responsibilities of an up-and-coming leader isn't to correct bad leadership. It's to **notice it without absorbing it**.

And it's harder than it sounds. Culture is learned through repetition, not instruction. The phrases you hear repeatedly begin to feel reasonable. The behaviors you once questioned start to look justified once you're tired, busy, or under pressure. What begins as observation slowly turns into permission.

That's the point of starting here.

When you notice bad leadership, you gain a choice. You can treat frustration as a signal to blame—or as a cue to get curious. You can explain gaps in performance by dismissing people, or you can look for what hasn't been taught, modeled, or made clear yet.

Leaders who later struggle with generational tension rarely became dismissive overnight. They arrived there gradually—one unexamined assumption at a time.

Up-and-coming leaders who mature well do something different. They remain attentive to the moments that make them uncomfortable. They ask why a phrase creates distance instead of clarity. They resist the urge to sound seasoned by sounding cynical. They understand that language reveals posture long before behavior confirms it.

Noticing bad leadership doesn't make you superior. It gives you responsibility—and the chance to choose differently.

You aren't obligated to fix everything you see yet. But you are responsible for what you carry forward. Every leader eventually becomes a reference point for others—an example used to explain what leadership looks like here. The habits you adopt now, quietly and consistently, will shape that reference.

Don't read this as a call-out of leaders who fall short. Read it as a marker: the moment leadership stops being abstract and becomes personal. The moment you realize how people are described matters as much as how work is assigned—and that culture is passed down less through mission statements than through everyday language.

The moment you notice bad leadership is not a setback.
It is an invitation.

An invitation to choose awareness over absorption.
To decide early whether you will repeat language that creates distance—or seek understanding that builds trust.

In the next chapter, we will examine one of the most common phrases that marks this moment of separation. Not to criticize it reflexively, but to understand what it signals, why it persists, and how easily well-intentioned leaders adopt it without realizing what it costs.

Before you decide what kind of leader you want to become, it helps to understand the stories leaders tell themselves about the people they lead.

In Practice

You're in a team meeting early in your career. The discussion turns to performance issues—missed deadlines, uneven quality, lack of follow-through. A senior leader leans back and says:

"This generation just doesn't have the same work ethic."

There's no argument. No one challenges it. A few people nod. The meeting moves on.

But something doesn't sit right.

You think about the people being referenced. You know some of them. You've worked alongside them. You've seen effort—maybe not always directed well, maybe not always consistent—but not absent. What you're hearing doesn't match what you've experienced.

You don't say anything. You're still learning the environment. Still figuring out where your voice fits. But you register the moment.

- What expectations were set?
- What support was provided?
- What clarity was missing?
- What changed that we didn't adjust for?

The label closed the loop.

The work continued—but understanding didn't.

What Strong Leaders Do

Strong leaders notice that moment—and pause internally, even if they don't interrupt externally.

- What specifically is not working?
- Where is the disconnect—skill, clarity, or expectation?
- What have we assumed instead of explained?
- What has changed that we haven't adjusted to?

They understand something critical:

When leaders generalize, they lose precision.
And when they lose precision, they lose influence.

Strong leaders resist the urge to sound experienced by sounding certain.

They stay curious longer.

They don't rush to defend the group being labeled, and they don't rush to agree with the leader speaking. Instead, they observe the gap between what's being said and what's actually happening.

That gap is where leadership begins to form.

Because over time, leaders are not remembered for how quickly they explained problems.

They are remembered for how well they understood them.

Apply This Now

You don't need authority to practice this.

Start here:

1. Catch the Label

The next time you hear a generalization (about a generation, a team, or a group), pause mentally.

Don't accept it automatically.
Ask yourself:

What specific behavior is this referring to?

2. Translate to Observation

Convert the label into something concrete.

- Are deadlines being missed?
- Are expectations unclear?
- Is feedback being understood?

Precision creates options.

3. Stay Curious in Conversation

If appropriate—and if the environment allows—ask one clarifying question:

"What specifically are we seeing that's driving that concern?"
You're not challenging the leader.

You're improving the conversation.

4. Decide What You Carry Forward

This is the most important step.

You will eventually be in the seat where someone looks to you for explanation.

Decide now:

Will you default to labels?

Or will you stay with understanding—even when it takes longer?

8

Noticing bad leadership is only the beginning.

What you do with what you notice is what shapes the leader you become.

Notice → Interpret → Practice → Prepare

NOTICE

What leadership moment in this chapter felt familiar to you?

INTERPRET

What might that moment reveal about how leadership culture is formed?

PRACTICE

Pay attention to one leadership moment this week—good or bad—and write down what it teaches you about how people want to be treated.

PREPARE

How would practicing this awareness shape the leader you are becoming?

CARRY FORWARD

Write one sentence from this chapter you want to keep close:

Chapter 2

What "This Generation" Really Means

By the time you hear the phrase *"this generation,"* something has already changed.

It rarely appears at the beginning of a conversation. It shows up later—after confusion, after missed expectations, after frustration has had time to settle. It sounds explanatory, even reasonable. A way to make sense of behavior that no longer fits familiar patterns.

But language is rarely just descriptive—especially in leadership.

When leaders say *"this generation,"* they are often not describing age or upbringing. They are naming a gap—between what they expect and what they are experiencing. Between how things used to work and how they work now. The phrase becomes a container for unresolved questions the leader has stopped asking.

If you're still becoming a leader, that phrase matters because it marks the moment curiosity gives way to categorization.

What began as an attempt to understand difference slowly becomes a way to manage discomfort. Complexity is reduced to shorthand. Individual behavior is flattened into group identity. And responsibility quietly shifts away from leadership systems toward the people least equipped to change them.

This is why the phrase feels distancing even when it is not intended to be dismissive. It creates an invisible boundary between *those who understand* and *those who need to catch up*. Once that boundary exists, development slows. Coaching becomes correction. Teaching becomes enforcement.

It is important to say this clearly: generational differences are real. They always have been. Values shift. Tools change. Context evolves. Every generation enters organizations shaped by conditions the previous one did not face. None of that is new.

What is new—or at least more visible—is how quickly leaders reach for labels instead of explanations.

For emerging leaders, this is an important moment to notice. Not because you need to challenge every senior leader who uses the phrase, but because you can learn what it often signals: someone has moved from *trying to understand* to *trying to cope*. And coping can feel productive, even when it keeps the real questions unanswered.

The issue isn't the phrase by itself. The issue is how easily it turns into a habit.

Once leaders begin using generational language to explain outcomes, it starts to shape expectations. Behavior is interpreted through the lens of assumption instead of context. Feedback becomes less precise. Opportunities narrow. People are managed based on what they represent rather than what they demonstrate.

People who are still earning their footing often sense this before they can articulate it. They notice that some people are given patience and others are given labels. That mistakes are treated differently depending on who makes them. That the same behavior can be seen as "initiative" in one person and "entitlement" in another.

What you are noticing is not favoritism. It is narrative.

Every organization runs on stories—about what success looks like, who can be trusted, and how much effort development is worth. *"This generation"* becomes one of those stories. And once a story takes hold, it quietly justifies decisions without being examined.

This is where the phrase becomes especially influential for leaders who are still forming their posture.

It offers an explanation without requiring growth. It sounds seasoned. It feels efficient. It allows leaders to move forward without adjusting how they teach, listen, or adapt. And because it is common, it feels safe to repeat.

But familiar language isn't the same as good leadership.

For up-and-coming leaders, the deeper risk isn't being labeled—it's starting to rely on labels yourself. Adopting them before you understand what they replace. Carrying them forward because they sound like experience rather than assumption.

The moment you stop asking *why* and start saying *who*, leadership has already narrowed.

This chapter isn't asking you to deny generational differences or pretend change is easy. It's asking you to notice when language becomes a stand-in for responsibility—when explanation turns into expectation, and leaders begin talking *about* people instead of *with* them.

Because that shift does not end with language.

Once leaders believe the story, they begin to feel justified in their frustration. They stop investing where they no longer expect return. And eventually, frustration hardens into something quieter, faster, and far more seductive.

By the time a leader reaches for *"this generation,"* the effort to understand has usually already thinned out. What started as a real question turns into a convenient explanation—language filling the space where curiosity used to stay.

For an emerging leader, that's the tell. The phrase offers clarity without ownership. It lets someone feel finished with the issue before they've done the work of naming what's actually unclear.

12

That's where leaders start to confuse naming with solving.

But a label isn't the same as understanding.

Quietly, the story shifts inside the leader: an explanation turns into an expectation, and frustration hardens into a belief that feels obvious.

That shift has a name.
And it can feel strangely efficient.

In Practice

You're part of a project that isn't gaining traction.

Deadlines are slipping. Communication feels uneven. Some team members are engaged, others seem disconnected. The work is getting done—but not well.

In a follow-up meeting, a senior leader summarizes the situation:

"They just don't communicate the way we used to. This generation expects everything to be handed to them."

Again, no one pushes back.

The conversation shifts toward enforcement—more check-ins, tighter controls, clearer consequences.

But something is missing.

Because when you look closer, what you see isn't a lack of capability. It's a mismatch:

- Expectations were assumed, not defined
- Feedback was given late, not early
- Communication styles weren't aligned
- Tools were different, but never reconciled

The team wasn't failing because of who they were.

They were struggling because of how the system was being run.

But the label made it easier to move on than to look deeper.

What Strong Leaders Do

Strong leaders recognize that generational language often appears when **leaders lose visibility into how work is actually happening**.

Instead of assuming the issue is the people, they examine the system around the people.

They ask:

- What does "good communication" actually look like here?

- Have we defined expectations—or just assumed them?

- Are we coaching behavior, or correcting outcomes?

- Are we adapting leadership, or expecting uniformity?

They understand a key principle:

Most performance gaps are not identity problems.
They are clarity, alignment, or development problems.

Strong leaders don't reject generational differences—they contextualize them.

They recognize:

- Communication preferences evolve

- Work expectations shift

- Feedback cycles change

- Technology reshapes interaction

But none of those changes remove the leader's responsibility to **teach, align, and adapt**.

14

Less effective leaders use generational language to stabilize themselves:

"This is just how they are."

Stronger leaders use it as a signal:

"Something here isn't connecting—what am I missing?"

That shift keeps leadership active instead of reactive.

Apply This Now

You don't need to wait until you're leading a team to practice this level of thinking.

Start with your current environment.

1. Replace Assumptions with Definitions

If something feels off, ask:

"What does success actually look like here?"

Not generally—specifically.

- What does "good communication" mean?
- What does "ownership" look like?
- What does "initiative" require?

Clarity reduces the need for labels.

2. Look for the System, Not the Symptom

When you see a pattern (missed deadlines, confusion, disengagement), ask:

- Is this a training issue?
- Is this an expectation issue?
- Is this a feedback timing issue?

Most issues repeat because the system allows them to.

3. Align Before You Correct

Before assuming someone is underperforming, check:

- Did they understand the expectation?
- Were they shown what "good" looks like?
- Did they get feedback early enough to adjust?

Correction without alignment creates frustration on both sides.

4. Decide How You Will Talk About People

This is a defining habit.

You will eventually describe others to:

- Your peers
- Your leaders
- Your team

Decide now:

Will your language:

- Reduce people to categories
  OR
- Clarify behavior and improve outcomes?

Because your language will shape how others are treated.

The moment you replace labels with understanding, leadership becomes more demanding—but far more effective.

And that effectiveness depends on something most leaders are tempted to trade away too early.

Notice → Interpret → Practice → Prepare

NOTICE

What language or labels did this chapter make you more aware of?

INTERPRET

What might those labels be replacing—curiosity, clarity, or responsibility?

PRACTICE

Replace one dismissive label you hear or use with a specific observation about behavior or context.

PREPARE

How does practicing precise language shape the leader you are becoming?

CARRY FORWARD

Capture one line you don't want to forget from this chapter:

Chapter 3

Why Cynicism Is a Leadership Shortcut

When leaders stop asking questions, they don't become neutral. They become efficient.

Cynicism rarely announces itself. It shows up as "realism"—a calm voice that sounds like it's been through enough to stop being surprised. It can feel like honesty. It can even feel like wisdom.

More often, though, cynicism is a shortcut—an easy way to settle a tension without doing the slower, more human work of understanding, coaching, or changing course. It lets a leader move forward without actually adjusting anything.

That's what makes it tricky when you're early in leadership. Cynicism doesn't look like failure; it can look like maturity. And once you start wearing it, it quietly reshapes how you judge people, how you coach, and who you decide is worth the effort.

That's the risk worth naming.

Cynicism isn't discernment. Discernment still does the work: it separates what can change from what can't without abandoning responsibility for either. Cynicism tends to skip that effort. It resolves tension by deciding the answer in advance.

You saw the external version of this in the last chapter. This is the internal one—faster, simpler, and far less curious.

When leaders adopt cynical explanations, they gain speed. Conversations shorten. Nuance disappears. Frustration starts to feel justified instead of unresolved. The organization keeps moving—but in a narrower direction.

This shortcut is tempting for one reason: it lowers the cost of disappointment.

Decide early that people are the problem and you no longer have to wrestle with systems that fall short. Decide that effort will not change outcomes and you no longer have to invest deeply. Cynicism feels efficient because it numbs you to the emotional weight leadership was always meant to carry.

Leadership was never meant to be effortless—especially emotionally.

The cost of cynicism is rarely immediate. It accumulates as low trust, stalled development, and an organization that quietly stops believing in its own future. Leaders who lean on cynicism often mistake stability for health.

At some point you'll feel the pull to sound seasoned—to trade curiosity for certainty, to reduce people to patterns instead of staying with the individual in front of you.

That's often when the habit starts to form.

The language of cynicism is subtle. It hides in phrases like *"That's just how it is,"* or *"You'll understand once you've been here longer."* It signals closure, not inquiry. It ends conversations instead of advancing them.

Cynicism can offer short-term relief.
Over time, it can make growth harder.

Leaders who grow well sit with unresolved questions longer. They resist simplifying before they understand. They accept that responsibility does not end just because answers are incomplete. Credibility comes less from explanations and more from continued engagement when things are difficult.

Cynicism chooses a direction.
It often pulls you away from responsibility.

If you're still growing, watch what happens when cynicism shows up. Everyone meets limits. The difference is whether that feeling becomes your default posture. Leaders who mature keep asking better questions instead of settling for faster answers.

The next chapter invites a replacement. Once you see cynicism as a shortcut, you get to decide what takes its place. The answer is not optimism. It is responsibility.

And responsibility, unlike cynicism, has to become yours in practice.

In Practice

You've been putting in consistent effort.

You prepare before meetings. You follow through on tasks. You try to communicate clearly. You take responsibility when things don't go perfectly.

But over time, you start to notice something:

Not everyone is operating the same way.

Some people do just enough to get by. Some miss details repeatedly. Some avoid accountability. And in certain situations, those patterns don't seem to carry consequences.

At first, you stay focused. You tell yourself:
"Just keep doing the right thing."

But the longer it continues, the more it wears on you.

You start to hear different language in conversations around you:

- "That's just how it is here."

- "Don't expect too much."

- "You'll understand after a while."

None of it sounds aggressive. It sounds experienced.

20

And slowly, almost without noticing, your internal dialogue begins to shift.

You stop asking:
"How can this improve?"

And start thinking:
"This probably won't change."

You still perform. You still contribute.

But something subtle has changed.

You've stopped expecting better.

That's where cynicism begins—not as a decision, but as an adjustment.

What Strong Leaders Do

Strong leaders recognize that cynicism often forms **in response to repeated friction without resolution**.

It is not always rooted in negativity.

It is often rooted in:

- Unmet expectations

- Inconsistent standards

- Lack of visibility into decision-making

- Effort that doesn't translate into outcomes

Instead of judging cynicism immediately, strong leaders examine what it's responding to.

But they do not stay there.

They understand something critical:

Cynicism feels like clarity—but it removes responsibility.

When leaders adopt cynical thinking, they gain speed—but lose influence.

Why?

Because cynicism:

- Closes questions early
- Reduces effort toward improvement
- Signals disengagement (even when performance remains high)
- Narrows how others experience your leadership

Strong leaders resist this by doing something that feels counterintuitive:

They **separate frustration from conclusion**.

They allow themselves to feel the friction—but they do not let that feeling define their interpretation.

Instead of saying:
"This won't change"

They ask:
"What part of this can I still influence?"

That question keeps leadership active.

Even in imperfect environments.

Even under constraint.

Even when progress is slow.

Because leadership is not defined by conditions—it is revealed by response.

Apply This Now

This is where discipline becomes visible.

You don't eliminate cynicism by pretending everything is fine.

You replace it by **choosing a more useful response**.

1. Name the Friction Clearly

When you feel cynical, pause and identify:

- What specifically is frustrating?
- What expectation is not being met?
- What pattern keeps repeating?

Clarity prevents emotional drift.

2. Separate Feeling from Conclusion

Instead of:
"This won't change"

Try:
"This is frustrating—but what is still within my control?"

This keeps your leadership engaged—even when outcomes are not.

3. Reclaim One Area of Ownership

Pick one area where you still have influence:

- Communication clarity
- Preparation
- Follow-up
- Supporting a teammate
- Asking better questions

Cynicism spreads when ownership shrinks.

Reverse that pattern.

4. Watch Your Language

Cynicism often shows up first in how you speak:

- "It doesn't matter anyway"
- "No one really cares"
- "That's just how things are"

These phrases don't just describe reality—they shape it.

Replace them with:

- "Here's what we can improve"
- "Here's what's not clear yet"
- "Here's where we can adjust"

Language either closes the loop—or keeps it open.

5. Decide What Kind of Leader You Will Be Under Pressure

This is the real test.

Not:

- When things are working
- When expectations are clear

But:

- When effort feels uneven
- When results don't match input
- When leadership around you falls short

Cynicism is easiest in those moments.

So is leadership.

Cynicism offers relief—but it limits what you're willing to build.

Responsibility does the opposite.

24

And responsibility, if you continue to carry it, will begin to shape how you show up—not just in how you think, but in how you engage others.

Chapter 3 Reflection

Notice → Interpret → Practice → Prepare

NOTICE
Where have you seen cynicism framed as experience or wisdom?

INTERPRET
What might cynicism be protecting someone from having to confront?

PRACTICE
When you feel cynical this week, pause and ask:
What responsibility am I avoiding by thinking this way?

PREPARE
How would resisting cynicism change how you show up as a leader?

CARRY FORWARD
Choose a sentence you'd want to remember on a hard day:

Deep-Dive Reflection (Optional)

Use this page when you want to go deeper than the chapter reflections.

Notice → Interpret → Practice → Prepare → Carry Forward

NOTICE

What is one leadership pattern you keep noticing—but haven't named clearly yet?

INTERPRET

What might be driving that pattern (pressure, incentives, unclear expectations, skill gaps, or something else)?

PRACTICE

What is one small action you can take this week to improve that pattern (clarify, coach, document, ask, or model)?

PREPARE

If you had to explain this issue to someone with more authority, what would you say in two clear sentences?

CARRY FORWARD

Write one sentence you want to remember when you feel tempted to disengage or get cynical:

PART II

CHOOSING YOUR LEADERSHIP POSTURE

In Part I, you learned how to notice leadership.

You started to see the pattern: language can create distance, shortcuts can replace curiosity, and frustration can reshape culture if no one interrupts it. That awareness matters—but awareness alone doesn't make you a leader.

Posture does.

Part II turns inward. It's about the default settings you reach for when leadership gets uncomfortable—before you have authority, protection, or certainty.

Every leader develops a posture long before they develop power.

Some learn to explain.
Some learn to blame.
Some learn to withdraw.
Some learn to perform.

Others learn to take responsibility.

This part of the book asks you to decide—intentionally—what posture you will practice as responsibility increases. Not later. Not once you are promoted. Now.

Because the habits you form when your influence is limited become the instincts that guide you when it expands.

Part II will challenge you to:

- Choose responsibility over explanation
- Remain teachable when frustration grows
- Disagree without eroding trust

These are not soft skills. They are leadership stabilizers. They determine whether your influence makes systems stronger—or more fragile.

This section may feel uncomfortable. That is intentional.

Posture is not revealed when things are easy. It is revealed when expectations collide with reality. When you do not control outcomes. When decisions are made above you. When your effort is not immediately rewarded.

How you respond in those moments is shaping the leader you are becoming.

By the end of Part II, you should feel more grounded—not because leadership has become easier, but because your response to it has become clearer.

Continue when you're ready.

It is time to stop watching leadership and start choosing how you will carry it.

Chapter 4

Blame or Responsibility

Once you see cynicism for what it is, a shortcut starts to stand out everywhere.

Not because leadership suddenly gets easier, but because the choice in front of you gets simpler.

Every leader, regardless of level, faces the same internal question: **Will I explain outcomes by assigning blame, or will I take responsibility for what I can influence?** You do not answer it once. You answer it repeatedly—in small moments long before anyone calls it leadership.

Blame is attractive because it feels explanatory. It answers *why* quickly. It assigns cause without requiring ownership—and it moves responsibility away from the self.

Responsibility does the opposite.

Responsibility begins with a harder truth: *I may not control this, but I am still accountable for how I respond.* That truth carries weight. It demands effort. It keeps you engaged when withdrawal would be easier.

This distinction matters early because it determines the posture you practice before authority amplifies it.

Blame sounds reasonable at first. It borrows the language of realism—constraints, limitations, external factors. *"If only they would..." "The system doesn't allow..." "That's above my level..."* Each line may be true. None of it builds leadership capacity on its own.

Responsibility asks a different question: *Given the reality I'm in, what is mine to own?*

That question does not ignore constraints. It works within them. It does not require authority; it requires intent.

Emerging leaders often underestimate how visible this posture is. People may not remember every result you deliver, but they remember how you explain outcomes. Over time, patterns form.

Leaders who rely on blame sound informed.
Leaders who choose responsibility sound trusted.

Responsibility is not absorbing fault for everything. It is refusing to outsource agency. It is recognizing that leadership grows when you stop at explanation and start asking, *What can I do from here?*—not because explanations are false, but because they are incomplete.

Many leaders retreat here because they assume responsibility means fixing everything. It does not. It means **clarifying what you can influence**, then acting consistently within that space.

Sometimes responsibility looks like asking a better question instead of offering an explanation. Sometimes it looks like preparing someone else instead of protecting your position. Sometimes it looks like saying, *"I didn't handle that well,"* and not rushing to justify it.

Blame protects your self-image in the moment.
Responsibility builds credibility over time.

This distinction also shapes how leaders view the people below them. Leaders who default to blame tend to treat performance gaps like character flaws. Leaders who practice responsibility treat gaps as information—about clarity, training, expectations, or support.

Compassion isn't the dividing line here. Ownership is.

For emerging leaders, this is where leadership turns participatory. You are no longer only noticing patterns or naming shortcuts. You are choosing how you will show up when outcomes fall short.

You will still feel frustration. You will still meet limits you cannot remove. Responsibility does not erase those realities; it refuses to let them define you.

Cynicism chose efficiency.
Responsibility chooses engagement.

The chapters ahead will build on this choice. They will explore how responsibility reshapes how you learn, how you disagree, how you use perspective, and eventually how you prepare others. This pivot is what makes the rest of the work usable.

Leadership does not begin when you are given authority.
It begins when you start deciding what is yours to own—right where you are.

In Practice

A project falls behind.

The timeline was aggressive, but it was accepted. Communication wasn't perfect, but updates were given. Several small issues compounded into one larger miss.

In the follow-up conversation, the explanations come quickly:

- "We didn't have enough time."

- "The requirements weren't clear."

- "We were waiting on input."

All of it is true.

No one is lying. No one is avoiding the facts.

But something is still missing.

The conversation explains what happened—but it doesn't move anything forward.

Everyone leaves with a shared understanding of the problem.

No one leaves with ownership of the solution.

And over time, that pattern becomes familiar.

What Strong Leaders Do

Strong leaders recognize the difference between **explaining outcomes** and **owning influence**.

They understand that explanations are necessary—but not sufficient.

Because explanation answers:

Why did this happen?

But leadership requires answering:

What is mine to improve?

That shift changes everything.

Instead of reinforcing the explanation, strong leaders redirect the conversation:

- "Given the timeline, what could we have clarified earlier?"

- "Where did communication break down—and how do we prevent that next time?"

- "What part of this process can we strengthen moving forward?"

They don't ignore constraints.

They work within them.

They understand a core principle:

Constraints don't remove responsibility.
They define where responsibility begins.

Less effective leaders use constraints to justify outcomes.

Stronger leaders use constraints to refine their approach.

That difference shows up over time.

Leaders who explain well may sound informed.

Leaders who take responsibility become trusted.

The Subtle Trap

Blame is not always obvious.

It doesn't always sound like:
"This is their fault."

More often, it sounds like:

- "That's just how the system works."

- "We weren't set up for success."

- "There wasn't much we could do."

Again—these statements can be true.

But when they become the end of the conversation, they quietly shift responsibility away from the leader.

This is the trap:

Explanation becomes a stopping point instead of a starting point.

And when that happens repeatedly, leadership stalls—even when effort remains high.

Apply This Now

You don't need authority to practice ownership.

You need clarity on what is yours.

1. Ask the Ownership Question

In any situation, ask:

"What part of this outcome is mine to influence?"

Not:

- "Who caused this?"
- "What went wrong?"

But:

- What is mine?

This keeps you engaged—even when control is limited.

2. Identify One Improvement Point

You don't need to fix everything.

Pick one:
- Clarify expectations earlier
- Communicate sooner
- Ask better questions
- Document decisions
- Follow up more consistently

Small ownership compounds.

3. Shift How You Speak About Outcomes

Instead of:

"We didn't have enough time"

Say:

"We need to clarify timelines earlier so we don't get compressed at the end"

Same reality—different posture.

34

One explains.

One improves.

4. Practice Visible Ownership

Ownership is not internal—it's observable.

This can look like:

- Acknowledging what could have been done better
- Offering a path forward
- Supporting adjustments—even if they weren't your idea

This builds credibility faster than performance alone.

5. Decide Early How You Will Lead Under Constraint

Every leader eventually faces:

- Limited resources
- Incomplete information
- External decisions

You cannot remove those conditions.

But you can decide:

Will you use them to explain outcomes?

Or to refine how you lead within them?

The moment you stop asking who is responsible—and start asking what is yours—you move from participation to leadership.

Chapter 4 Reflection

Notice → Interpret → Practice → Prepare

NOTICE
Where have you seen blame presented as realism or experience?

INTERPRET
What responsibility might be hidden behind those explanations?

PRACTICE
In one situation you do not control, identify **one action** you can still take that improves the outcome.

PREPARE
How does choosing responsibility—even in small ways—prepare you for greater leadership?

CARRY FORWARD
What's one sentence from this chapter you'd quote back to yourself?

Responsibility is not heavy—it is clarifying.

Chapter 5

Learning Without Becoming Bitter

Choosing responsibility changes how you see your role.
It also exposes a new risk.

When you stop blaming circumstances and start owning what you can influence, you notice more: constraints, inconsistencies, decisions that still don't add up. Responsibility sharpens your sight. Without care, that clarity can slide into bitterness.

It doesn't start loud. Usually it starts as disappointment. You prepare, you invest, you try to do it the right way—and then a decision gets made above you that you don't agree with or can't fully see. Effort doesn't always get recognized. Progress doesn't always feel fair.

For an emerging leader, these are some of the most formative moments you'll face.

Bitterness forms when responsibility is practiced without perspective—when effort is treated like a guarantee, when you expect clarity before you have context, and when you mistake incomplete information for incompetence.

The temptation is understandable. You are close enough to see problems but far enough from authority to feel powerless. That gap can feel personal even when it is structural.

This is a place where even capable leaders can lose momentum.

They keep performing, but they stop learning. They comply without curiosity. They grow quieter—not because they matured, but because they withdrew. Over time, self-protection can start to resemble wisdom.

Learning requires openness.
Bitterness makes it harder to stay open.

Leaders who grow well do something counterintuitive here: they assume there is more context than they can see. Not to excuse poor decisions, but to stay humble. They remain curious even when frustrated. They seek understanding without demanding agreement.

To be clear, this isn't an argument for tolerating dysfunction or silencing concerns. It's a reminder that incomplete perspective isn't the same as bad intent—and that you can stay teachable even when advancement feels slow.

Leaders who avoid bitterness learn to separate **disagreement from disengagement**. You can question a decision without questioning your place. You can learn from leaders you do not fully admire. You can extract insight from imperfect examples without adopting their flaws.

This is where responsibility deepens.

Responsibility is not only about what you own. It is also about what you are willing to learn—even when learning feels unfair.

Bitterness can make growth feel like something others owe you. Learning keeps growth in your hands—something you pursue. Over time, that difference shows up in how leaders speak, how they listen, and how much responsibility others trust them with.

Over time, leaders tend to notice this posture. Not because they agree with everything you say, but because they recognize resilience. Leaders who stay curious under pressure often signal readiness for more responsibility. When leaders grow bitter, pressure can start to narrow what they're able to see.

This chapter isn't telling you to suppress frustration. It's about shaping it—turning disappointment into data instead of identity, and resisting the urge to define yourself by what hasn't been given to you yet.

The next chapter will explore how this posture shows up in disagreement—how to respect authority without surrendering conviction. Because learning without bitterness prepares you not just to endure leadership, but to engage it honestly.

In Practice

You've been doing the work.

You prepare. You take responsibility. You stay engaged. You've made the shift from explanation to ownership—and it shows.

But over time, something else begins to surface.

A decision gets made above you that you don't fully understand.
An opportunity you were prepared for goes in a different direction.
A leader you respect makes a call that doesn't align with what you expected.

You stay professional. You continue to perform.

But internally, the questions start to build:

- "Why wasn't that handled differently?"
- "What am I missing?"
- "Does this actually matter as much as I thought?"

At first, those questions are productive.

But if they go unanswered long enough, they begin to change tone.

They shift from curiosity to conclusion.

And that's where bitterness begins—not as an outburst, but as a quiet adjustment in how you interpret your environment.

You don't disengage.

But you stop leaning in the same way.

What Strong Leaders Do

Strong leaders understand that **bitterness is often a signal—not a failure**.

It signals:

- A gap between expectation and reality
- A lack of visibility into decision-making
- A misalignment between effort and outcome

But they also understand the risk:

If left unexamined, bitterness changes how you show up—long before it changes what you do.

That's why strong leaders do something that feels counterintuitive:

They **process frustration without letting it define their posture**.

They don't ignore it.

They don't suppress it.

They examine it.

Instead of asking:
"Why did this happen to me?"

They ask:
"What am I assuming that I may not fully understand yet?"

This doesn't mean they agree with every decision.

40

It means they refuse to let incomplete understanding turn into fixed judgment.

They recognize:

Limited visibility is not the same as poor leadership.

And they remain open to the possibility that:

- There is context they don't have
- There are trade-offs they don't see
- There are constraints they haven't experienced yet

This posture keeps them teachable—even when they disagree.

The Turning Point

Bitterness becomes a problem when it shifts from:

A reaction to a situation

Into:

A lens you use to interpret everything

That shift is subtle.

You start to:

- Expect decisions to be flawed
- Assume effort won't be recognized
- Interpret ambiguity as incompetence
- Withdraw investment slightly—just enough to protect yourself

You still perform.

But you stop growing at the same rate.

Because growth requires openness—and bitterness reduces it.

Strong leaders catch that shift early.

Not by eliminating frustration.

But by refusing to let it become their default perspective.

Apply This Now

This is where leadership becomes internal discipline.

1. Identify the Source of Frustration

Instead of generalizing, get specific:

- What expectation was not met?
- What outcome didn't align with your effort?
- What decision felt unclear?

Precision keeps frustration from becoming identity.

2. Separate Outcome from Interpretation

What happened:
"The decision didn't go my way."

Interpretation (optional, but powerful):
"This must not matter."

Strong leaders challenge the second part.

3. Seek Context Before Conclusion

If possible, ask:

- "Can you help me understand the reasoning behind that decision?"
- "What factors influenced that outcome?"

Not to challenge—but to learn.

Even partial context changes perspective.

4. Stay Invested Where You Have Influence

Bitterness often shows up as withdrawal.

Reverse that pattern.

Double down on:

- Your preparation
- Your communication
- Your development of others
- Your consistency

This keeps your leadership active—even when your environment is imperfect.

5. Decide What You Will Learn from Imperfect Leadership

This is one of the most important habits you can build.

Ask:

- What is working here?
- What would I do differently?
- What am I learning about leadership under pressure?

You don't need perfect examples to grow.

You need honest observation.

Learning without bitterness doesn't make leadership easier.

It makes your growth sustainable.

And that sustainability becomes visible in how you engage—not just with the work, but with the people around you.

Chapter 5 Reflection

Notice → Interpret → Practice → Prepare

NOTICE
Where have you seen frustration quietly turn into withdrawal or bitterness?

INTERPRET
What expectations might be fueling that bitterness?

PRACTICE
Identify one leader you struggle to respect and extract **one skill or lesson** worth learning from them.

PREPARE
How does staying teachable under frustration prepare you for greater responsibility?

CARRY FORWARD

Note one sentence worth carrying into your week:

Chapter 6

Respect Is Not Agreement

A common early misread is thinking respect requires agreement.
Not necessarily.

In fact, some of the most respected leaders are those who disagree clearly, calmly, and consistently—without turning difference into defiance or silence into compliance. The skill is not avoiding disagreement; it is **how disagreement is handled when power is uneven**.

This matters because leadership environments are full of decisions you will not control and strategies you will not fully endorse. If respect depends on agreement, your credibility will rise and fall with every decision you dislike. Over time, that makes you harder to trust—not because you care too much, but because your steadiness becomes inconsistent.

Respect is a posture.
Agreement is a position.

The two get confused because disagreement feels risky early on. People worry about being seen as difficult, disloyal, or naïve. In response, many default to one of two unproductive extremes: silent compliance or reactive challenge. Neither builds trust.

Silent compliance can be read as disengagement.
Reactive challenge can be read as defensiveness.

Respectful disagreement requires something harder: discipline.

Discipline in how you frame concerns. Discipline in when you raise them. Discipline in accepting that being heard does not guarantee being followed. Leaders who master this discipline earn credibility because they show they can engage complexity without destabilizing the system.

This is where responsibility and learning converge.

Leaders who practice responsibility own their role in the outcome—even when their recommendation is not adopted. Leaders who avoid bitterness remain open to understanding decisions they disagree with. Respectful disagreement is the visible expression of both.

For emerging leaders, the test is not whether you have an opinion—it is whether your opinion strengthens the conversation or narrows it.

Respectful disagreement starts with understanding. Before challenging a decision, strong leaders can articulate the reasoning behind it accurately. Not as a performance, but as proof that they listened. This builds trust even when consensus is not possible.

Next comes clarity. Respectful disagreement is specific. It focuses on impact, risk, or alignment—not on personalities or intent. It avoids absolutes. It acknowledges trade-offs. It recognizes constraints.

Finally comes acceptance. Once a decision is made, respect shows up in how you support execution. This is where it helps to stay coherent: avoid quietly undermining what you were allowed to influence, and avoid distancing yourself from outcomes you helped shape. Stay accountable.

This is a common place to slip.

A common misstep is assuming that voicing disagreement entitles you to disown the result. Credibility tends to grow when people see you support decisions you questioned—without drifting into passive resistance or disengagement.

Respect does not mean silence.
It means coherence.

Learn this early and you become a trusted intermediary. You can translate between perspectives. You can surface risk without triggering defensiveness. You can represent the organization upward and downward without distortion.

This is also where generational tension often dissolves.

Leaders who respect without requiring agreement are less likely to dismiss perspectives that challenge them. They understand that disagreement often carries insight—especially from those closer to the work or newer to the system. Respectful leaders remain open without surrendering standards.

This chapter completes the posture shift begun earlier in the book. You have moved from noticing leadership, to rejecting shortcuts, to choosing responsibility, to remaining teachable. Now you add a critical capability: **engaging difference without losing trust**.

Learning to disagree respectfully isn't the end of leadership growth.
It's the threshold.

Once you can hold responsibility without bitterness and express disagreement without eroding trust, something changes. People experience you as steadier under pressure. Your perspective begins to carry more weight.

From there, the question isn't whether you can engage difference—it's whether you know what to do with the perspective you bring.

Contribution earns you a seat inside.

In Practice

A decision is made that you don't agree with.

You've done the analysis. You've thought through the risks. You've seen how similar situations played out before. From your perspective, there's a better way forward.

48

But you are not the final decision-maker.

The direction is set.

Now you're left with a choice—not about the decision itself, but about how you respond to it.

You've likely seen both extremes before.

One person stays quiet in the meeting, nods along, and later says: "I didn't agree with that at all."

Another pushes back aggressively in the moment, challenges the leader publicly, and creates tension that shifts the focus from the issue to the interaction.

Both responses feel understandable.

Neither builds long-term trust.

The first creates distance.

The second creates friction.

And both send the same underlying signal:

"I don't know how to engage disagreement productively."

That's the gap this chapter is meant to close.

What Strong Leaders Do

Strong leaders understand that disagreement is not the problem.

How disagreement is handled is the signal.

They approach disagreement with three disciplines:

1. They Understand Before They Challenge

Before offering a counterpoint, strong leaders ensure they can accurately explain the current position.

Not to agree with it—but to prove they understand it.

They might say:

"Let me make sure I'm tracking this correctly—are we prioritizing speed here over long-term stability?"

This does two things:

- It reduces defensiveness
- It shows respect for the decision process

And it ensures they are challenging the **actual decision**, not a misunderstanding of it.

2. They Frame Disagreement Around Impact, Not Opinion

Weak disagreement sounds like:
"I don't think that's the right approach."

Strong disagreement sounds like:
"One risk we may want to consider is how this impacts downstream coordination."

The difference is discipline.

Strong leaders:

- Focus on outcomes
- Highlight trade-offs

- Avoid personal language
- Stay specific

They don't argue to be right.

They contribute to make the decision better.

3. They Stay Aligned After the Decision

This is where credibility is either built—or lost.

Once a decision is made, strong leaders:

- Support execution
- Clarify direction for others
- Stay consistent in messaging

They don't:

- Undermine the decision quietly
- Distance themselves from the outcome
- Signal disagreement through disengagement

They understand:

You can disagree in the process and still be aligned in execution.

That combination builds trust faster than agreement ever will.

The Hidden Test

Respectful disagreement is not tested when:

- The stakes are low

- The environment is safe
- The outcome doesn't matter much

It's tested when:

- You care deeply about the outcome
- You believe the decision is flawed
- You don't control the final call

That's where posture becomes visible.

Because in those moments, you are not just communicating a point.

You are demonstrating:

- Emotional discipline
- Professional maturity
- Leadership readiness

And people notice.

Apply This Now

This is a skill you can practice immediately.

1. Practice Clarifying Before Responding

In your next disagreement, start with:

"Can I confirm I'm understanding this correctly?"

This alone will improve most conversations.

2. Focus on One Risk, Not Ten Opinions

Instead of listing everything you disagree with, identify:

- One key concern
- One potential impact
- One alternative

Clarity beats volume.

3. Control Tone as Much as Content

What you say matters.

How you say it determines whether it's heard.

Stay:

- Calm
- Direct
- Measured

Tone signals intent.

4. Stay Consistent After the Decision

Once direction is set:

- Communicate it clearly
- Support the outcome
- Help others execute

Do not:

- Re-litigate the decision
- Signal disagreement through behavior

Consistency builds credibility.

5. Decide What You Want to Be Known For

Over time, people will associate you with one of three patterns:

- Avoids disagreement
- Creates tension
- Strengthens conversations

Choose deliberately.

Because your reputation will form from repeated moments like this.

Respectful disagreement is not about winning a conversation.

It's about earning trust in the moments when alignment is not automatic.

Chapter 6 Reflection

Notice → Interpret → Practice → Prepare

NOTICE
Where have you seen disagreement handled well—or poorly?

INTERPRET
What did those examples reveal about trust and respect?

PRACTICE
In your next disagreement, articulate the other person's position accurately **before** stating your own.

PREPARE
How does learning to disagree respectfully prepare you for broader responsibility?

CARRY FORWARD
Write one line you want to keep practicing:

Respectful disagreement is where perspective becomes contribution.

PART II CHECKPOINT - INTEGRATION

Up to this point, nothing in this book has required authority.

It has required something more demanding:
awareness, discipline, and choice.

In Part I, you learned to notice leadership.

In Part II, you were asked to decide how you will carry it.

That decision is not theoretical.

It is already showing up in how you:

- respond to friction
- interpret decisions
- speak about others
- manage your own reactions

You may not control outcomes yet.

But you are already shaping how leadership feels to the people around you.

And that matters more than most leaders realize early enough.

Because posture becomes pattern.

And pattern becomes reputation.

Before moving forward, pause here—not to assess what you know, but to assess what you are practicing.

Before You Move Forward

Part II was not about collecting ideas.

It was about changing how you carry responsibility.

Before you continue, take a moment to assess what is actually shifting—not just what makes sense.

The way you carry responsibility now will define how others experience your leadership later.

1. Posture Check

Which shift in Part II challenged you the most?

☐ Choosing responsibility instead of explanation

☐ Staying teachable under frustration

☐ Disagreeing without eroding trust

Why do you think that one was hardest?

2. Language Audit

What language have you noticed yourself using more carefully since starting this section?
(About leadership, decisions, people, or the organization.)

3. Responsibility in Practice

Where have you already chosen responsibility over blame—however small?

What changed because of that choice?

4. Frustration Awareness

What has frustrated you recently—and how did you handle it differently than you might have before?

5. Respect Under Pressure

Think of a moment you disagreed with someone in authority. How did you approach it?

☐ With silence

☐ With reaction

☐ With discipline

☐ With curiosity

What would you repeat—or do differently next time?

6. Identity Formation

Write the sentence below as plainly as you can:

Compared to when I started this book, I am beginning to see myself as a leader who…

7. Readiness Question

If your responsibility increased tomorrow, which posture from Part II would you need to strengthen first?

Closing Prompt

You do not move forward because you understand more.

You move forward because you carry responsibility differently.

If that shift has started, continue.

Part III will ask you to use what you see—not for yourself, but for the organization.

Leadership is already forming in you. The question is whether you are shaping it—or letting it shape you.

PART III

PERSPECTIVE AS CONTRIBUTION

Part III is where your perspective starts to travel.

You have spent the first part of this book learning how to carry yourself. You learned to notice leadership without absorbing its flaws. You rejected shortcuts that feel efficient but erode responsibility. You practiced staying teachable under frustration and learned how to disagree without breaking trust. Those chapters were not about standing out—they were about becoming stable.

Now the work changes.

What you notice starts to matter once it's translated into something others can use.

Every up-and-coming leader has perspective. You see how work actually happens. You feel friction where systems strain. You notice gaps between intention and execution. That awareness is not accidental—it is positional. But perspective alone does not create value.

Contribution does.

Contribution is perspective translated into something the organization can use. It is insight shaped by context, delivered with discipline, and offered in service of outcomes larger than yourself. It is not about being right. It is about being useful.

This part of the book asks more of you.

Not just to see clearly.
Not just to carry yourself well.
But to convert what you see into something that improves how people work, grow, and lead.

By this point, leadership is no longer something you are observing or preparing for.

It is something you are practicing in real time.

What you see must now become useful.
What you carry must now create value.

This is where leadership begins to extend beyond you.

Because the final responsibility of a leader is not simply to perform—but to multiply.

Chapter 7

Perspective Is Not Power

Seeing clearly does not make you influential.

It can feel like it should. When you begin to notice patterns others miss—inefficiencies, misalignment, gaps in communication—it is natural to assume that clarity should translate into impact. But in most organizations, it does not work that way.

Perspective is common.

Useful perspective is rare.

Many people see problems. Fewer people know how to translate what they see into something others can act on. Fewer still can do it in a way that builds trust instead of resistance.

This is where many emerging leaders stall.

They notice more—but influence does not increase. Frustration follows. It becomes tempting to believe the issue is positional: *If I had the authority, I would fix this.*

Sometimes that is true.

More often, the gap is not authority.

It is translation.

Raw perspective can feel sharp, but if it is not shaped, it lands as criticism. If it is not timed well, it feels disruptive. If it is not connected to shared outcomes, it can be dismissed—even when it is correct.

Leadership is not measured by what you see.

It is measured by what changes because of how you communicate it.

This requires discipline.

Discipline to understand context before speaking.
Discipline to align your message with priorities others are responsible for.
Discipline to deliver insight in a way that invites engagement instead of defensiveness.

It also requires patience.

Influence rarely expands at the same speed as awareness. You may see clearly long before others are ready to act. That gap can feel frustrating if you interpret it as being ignored. It becomes productive when you treat it as a signal to refine how you contribute.

The goal is not to prove you are right.

The goal is to make what you see usable.

That shift—from expression to contribution—is where perspective begins to matter.

In Practice

You're in a meeting where something isn't working.

The discussion circles the same issue. The same points are repeated. Progress is slow. You can see the disconnect—what's missing, what's unclear, what isn't being said directly.

And in your head, the solution feels obvious.

You've seen this before. You understand the friction. You know what would improve the situation.

But you hesitate.

Not because you don't have a perspective.

Because you're not sure how it will land.

So, you stay quiet.

Or you offer something partial—just enough to contribute without fully stepping forward.

The meeting ends.

The issue remains.

And you leave knowing:
You had something useful—but it didn't get used.

That moment is more common than most leaders admit.

And it reveals an important truth:

Having perspective is not the same as creating impact.

What Strong Leaders Do

Strong leaders understand that **perspective only matters when it becomes usable**.

Not just accurate.

Not just insightful.

Usable.

They focus less on what they see—and more on how they translate what they see into something others can act on.

They recognize three common failure points:

1. Perspective That Is Not Shared

Some leaders see clearly but stay silent.

They assume:

- It's not their place
- Someone else will say it
- The timing isn't right

Over time, this creates a gap between awareness and contribution.

Strong leaders close that gap.

2. Perspective That Is Not Structured

Others share—but without clarity.

They speak in fragments:

- Observations without direction
- Concerns without framing
- Ideas without connection to outcomes

The insight may be correct—but it's hard to use.

Strong leaders structure their thinking before they share it.

3. Perspective That Is Not Aligned

Some perspectives are shared clearly—but not in a way that connects to the group's goals.

They sound like:

- Personal opinions
- Isolated ideas
- Standalone critiques

Strong leaders align their perspective to:

- The objective
- The outcome
- The team's priorities

This makes their input easier to adopt.

The Shift

This is where leadership matures.

You move from:

"I see the problem"

To:

"I can help move this forward"

That shift changes how others experience you.

Because leadership is not measured by:

- What you notice
- What you think

- What you believe

It is measured by:

What becomes better because you spoke.

Apply This Now

You can begin practicing contribution immediately.

1. Translate Insight into Action

Before you speak, ask:

"What does this improve?"

If your perspective doesn't move something forward, refine it until it does.

2. Use Simple Structure

When sharing, use:

- Observation → "Here's what I'm seeing…"
- Impact → "Here's what that affects…"
- Suggestion → "Here's one way we could improve it…"

This makes your thinking usable.

3. Match Timing to the Moment

Not every insight needs to be delivered immediately.

Strong leaders assess:

- Is this the right setting?

- Is this the right moment?
- Is this the right level of detail?

Timing increases effectiveness.

4. Start Where You Are

You don't need authority to contribute.

Start with:

- Clarifying confusion
- Connecting ideas
- Simplifying complexity
- Asking better questions

Contribution begins before recognition.

5. Decide to Be Useful

This is the defining shift.

In every interaction, ask:

"How can I make this better?"

Not:

- "Was I heard?"
- "Did I sound right?"

But:

- Did I improve something?

That mindset builds influence over time.

You've stopped expecting better.

Perspective earns attention.

Contribution earns trust.

And trust is what allows your leadership to grow beyond your position.

Chapter 7 Reflection

Notice → Interpret → Practice → Prepare

NOTICE

Where have you seen strong insight fail to create change?

INTERPRET

What might have been missing—timing, framing, or alignment?

PRACTICE

Take one observation you've had recently and rewrite it as something actionable.

PREPARE

How does shaping your perspective increase your influence?

CARRY FORWARD

Perspective matters when it becomes usable.

Seeing clearly is not enough.
It must become useful.

Chapter 8

Making Your Perspective Useful

Once you understand that perspective alone is not enough, the next question becomes:

What makes it useful?

Usefulness in leadership is not accidental. It is built through three disciplines: timing, framing, and alignment.

Timing determines whether your insight can be heard. Even accurate observations can be ignored if they arrive at the wrong moment—when decisions are already made, when priorities are fixed, or when attention is elsewhere. Leaders who contribute effectively learn to read when input is most valuable, not just when it feels urgent to share.

Framing determines how your insight is received. The same idea can create resistance or engagement depending on how it is presented. Framing focuses on impact, not frustration. It connects what you see to outcomes others care about—mission success, team performance, risk reduction, or clarity of execution.

Alignment determines whether your contribution moves forward. Insight that operates outside of organizational priorities rarely gains traction. Leaders who contribute well understand how their observations fit within larger objectives. They do not dilute their perspective—they position it.

This is where discipline becomes visible.

It is easier to say what you see than to shape it. Easier to point out gaps than to connect them to outcomes. Easier to speak from frustration than from intent.

But useful leaders do the harder work.

They translate.

Instead of saying, "This process doesn't work," they clarify
where it breaks and what outcome it affects.
Instead of saying, "Communication is poor," they identify what is
unclear and what decisions are being delayed.
Instead of pointing out problems, they offer direction.

This does not mean you always have the full solution.

It means you take responsibility for making your perspective
actionable.

Over time, people begin to notice this difference. They may not
agree with every point you raise, but they recognize that your
input moves conversations forward instead of stalling them.

That is how influence grows.

Not by volume.
Not by position.
But by usefulness.

In Practice

You're in a working session where things are starting to drift.

The objective is clear on paper—but in practice, the conversation
is scattered. People are talking past each other. Some are focused
on details, others on direction. Progress feels slow.

You recognize the issue quickly:

There's no shared clarity.

You've seen this before. You know what would help:

- Simplifying the objective
- Aligning on priorities
- Structuring the next steps

So, you speak up.

You say:
"I think we just need to get more aligned."

Heads nod.

But nothing changes.

The conversation continues the same way.

And that's the moment many leaders miss:

The problem wasn't your perspective.
The problem was that it wasn't specific enough to act on.

You were right.

But your input wasn't usable.

What Strong Leaders Do

Strong leaders understand that usefulness requires **precision**.

They don't stop at identifying the issue.

They translate it into something others can immediately apply.

Instead of saying:
"We need more alignment"

They say:
"Let's take two minutes to clarify the objective—are we prioritizing speed or accuracy for this phase?"

That difference matters.

Because:

- It defines the problem
- It narrows the focus
- It creates a next step

Strong leaders operate with a simple principle:

If people don't know what to do next, your perspective isn't finished.

Making Perspective Actionable

To make your contribution useful, it must do at least one of the following:

1. Clarify Direction

Help people understand:

- What matters most
- What success looks like
- What the priority is

Example:
"Before we move forward, can we confirm what outcome we're optimizing for here?"

2. Simplify Complexity

When discussions become layered or unclear, strong leaders reduce noise.

Example:
"It sounds like we're solving three different problems—can we isolate the first one and move step by step?"

3. Create Next Steps

Contribution becomes real when it produces movement.

Example:
"Based on this, the next step could be assigning one owner to define the timeline by tomorrow."

4. Connect the Dots

Sometimes the value is not new insight—it's connecting existing ones.

Example:
"This ties back to what we discussed earlier about communication gaps—this may be where that's showing up again."

The Discipline of Specificity

General statements feel safe.

Specific statements create movement.

Compare:

"We need to improve communication"

vs.

"We need to define who owns updates and how often they happen"

One is correct.

The other is actionable.

Strong leaders choose actionable.

Apply This Now

This is where your contribution becomes visible.

1. Replace General Language with Specific Action

Catch yourself when you say:

- "We should improve…"
- "We need to focus on…"
- "We should align on…"

And refine it:

- What exactly should change?
- Who owns it?
- By when?

2. Add a Next Step to Every Insight

Before speaking, ask:

"What does someone do with this?"

If the answer is unclear—refine your input.

3. Use Short, Structured Input

Keep it simple:

- "Here's what I'm seeing…"
- "Here's what that affects…"
- "Here's one step we could take…"

This increases clarity and reduces resistance.

4. Watch the Impact of Your Contribution

After you speak, observe:

- Did the conversation move forward?
- Did clarity improve?
- Did people take action?

That feedback loop helps you refine your effectiveness.

5. Build a Reputation for Usefulness

Over time, people begin to associate you with one of two patterns:

- Adds noise
- Adds clarity

Strong leaders become known for the second.

Because they consistently make things easier to understand and act on.

When your perspective consistently creates clarity and movement, something changes.

People don't just hear you.

They begin to rely on you.

Chapter 8 Reflection

Notice → Interpret → Practice → Prepare

NOTICE
Where have you seen ideas gain traction—and where have they stalled?

INTERPRET
What made the difference in how they were delivered?

PRACTICE
Take a current issue and frame it in terms of impact and outcome.

PREPARE
How does usefulness shape how others respond to you?

CARRY FORWARD
Useful leaders move work forward.

Usefulness creates movement.

Consistency sustains it.

Chapter 9

From Observation to Contribution

At some point, awareness becomes responsibility.

Not because you are in charge—but because you can see what others may not yet be acting on.

This is where leadership becomes participatory.

You are no longer just interpreting the environment. You are shaping it—through what you say, what you reinforce, and what you choose to act on consistently.

Contribution begins with a simple shift:

From noticing friction
to reducing it.

Friction shows up in many forms:

- Unclear expectations

- Repeated misunderstandings

- Delays caused by missing information

- Gaps between intent and execution

Most people experience friction.

Fewer people take responsibility for improving it.

Contribution does not require authority to begin. It starts with small, consistent actions:

Clarifying what is unclear before confusion spreads.
Sharing information that helps others move faster.
Bringing alignment to conversations that are drifting.
Supporting decisions once they are made—even if you
questioned them.

These actions are easy to overlook because they do not look like
leadership at scale.

But they are.

They shape how work gets done. They build trust. They reduce
the cost of coordination across a team or organization.

Over time, contribution compounds.

People begin to rely on you—not because of your title, but
because of your consistency. Your presence starts to signal
progress. Conversations move forward when you are part of
them. Execution becomes clearer.

This is when something important shifts.

You stop being seen only as someone who performs.

You start being seen as someone who improves how others
perform.

That is the beginning of leadership impact.

In Practice

You've started contributing more consistently.

You're not just observing—you're clarifying, simplifying, and
helping move conversations forward. People are beginning to

notice. Your input is being acknowledged. Sometimes it even shapes decisions.

But something still feels uneven.

In one meeting, your perspective lands well.

In another, it doesn't seem to go anywhere.

In some situations, people lean in when you speak.

In others, your input gets acknowledged—and then ignored.

Nothing is wrong.

But nothing feels consistent yet.

This is the stage many leaders misunderstand.

They assume:
"If I'm right, it should always work."

But leadership doesn't operate that way.

Because influence is not just about being right.

It's about being **reliable over time**.

What Strong Leaders Do

Strong leaders understand that **influence is built through repetition, not moments**.

They don't measure effectiveness by whether one idea is accepted.

They measure it by whether their presence consistently improves the environment.

They focus on three patterns:

1. Consistency of Contribution

Strong leaders don't contribute occasionally—they contribute predictably.

They:

- Show up prepared
- Speak with clarity
- Add value regularly

This creates familiarity.

And familiarity builds trust.

2. Consistency of Tone

People don't just respond to what you say.

They respond to:

- How you say it
- When you say it
- How you show up under pressure

Strong leaders maintain:

- Composure
- Clarity
- Professional discipline

Even when:

- They disagree
- They're frustrated
- They're under pressure

This creates stability.

And stability builds credibility.

3. Consistency of Follow-Through

This is where many leaders lose momentum.

They contribute in the moment—but don't reinforce it afterward.

Strong leaders:

- Follow up
- Clarify next steps
- Support execution

They understand:

Contribution creates momentum.
Follow-through sustains it.

The Compounding Effect

Influence rarely shows up as a sudden shift.

It builds gradually.

- One useful comment
- One clarified direction

- One improved conversation

Over time, these stack.

And people begin to think:

- "They make things clearer"
- "They help move things forward"
- "They're consistent"

That perception matters.

Because once people begin to expect value from you, they start to:

- Listen earlier
- Ask for input
- Include you in decisions

That's how influence grows.

The Misconception

Many emerging leaders believe:

"I need authority to have consistent impact."

But what they actually need is:

Consistency in how they contribute.

Authority amplifies influence.

It doesn't create it.

Apply This Now

This is where your leadership becomes visible over time.

1. Focus on Patterns, Not Moments

After each interaction, don't ask:

"Did that go well?"

Ask:

"Am I showing up consistently the same way?"

Consistency builds identity.

2. Build a Contribution Rhythm

Decide:

- How you prepare
- When you speak
- How you follow up

Make it repeatable.

3. Reinforce Your Contributions

After a meeting:

- Send a summary
- Clarify next steps
- Support execution

This turns input into impact.

4. Watch How Others Respond Over Time

Look for patterns:

- Are people asking for your input more often?
- Are you being included earlier?
- Are your ideas gaining traction faster?

That's influence developing.

5. Decide What You Want to Be Known For

Over time, your consistency creates your reputation.

You will become known as someone who:

- Adds clarity
- Creates momentum
- Strengthens conversations

Or not.

That identity is built through repetition.

Influence is not built in a single moment.

It is built in how consistently you show up—and how reliably you make things better.

Chapter 9 Reflection

Notice → Interpret → Practice → Prepare
NOTICE
Where do you see recurring friction in your environment?

INTERPRET
What might be causing that friction beneath the surface?

PRACTICE
Take one small action this week to reduce friction for others.

PREPARE
How does reducing friction build trust in your leadership?

CARRY FORWARD
Contribution begins with improving what is already in front of you.

Contribution builds trust.

Trust expands your reach.

Chapter 10

Earning Trust at Scale

Trust is not built in statements.

It is built in patterns.

By the time you reach this stage, your leadership is no longer defined only by isolated actions. People are starting to form expectations about you. They anticipate how you will respond under pressure. They predict how you will handle responsibility.

That pattern is your credibility.

Credibility is what allows trust to scale.

Without it, influence remains limited to direct interaction. With it, your leadership extends beyond your presence. Decisions move faster because people trust how you think. Teams align more easily because they trust how you operate.

This is where consistency becomes non-negotiable.

Not perfection—consistency.

Consistency in how you communicate.
Consistency in how you follow through.
Consistency in how you handle pressure.
Consistency in how you treat people—especially when it is difficult.

Inconsistency creates hesitation.

Hesitation slows everything down.

Leaders who earn trust at scale reduce that hesitation. They become a stabilizing force. People know what to expect—not because everything is predictable, but because your principles are.

This also means your leadership is now visible in new ways.

People are learning from you without direct instruction. They are modeling how you speak, how you prioritize, how you respond to setbacks. Your behavior is becoming a reference point.

This is where leadership moves beyond execution.

It becomes example.

And example, over time, becomes culture.

In Practice

You've built a pattern.

You contribute consistently. You bring clarity. You follow through. People trust your input in the rooms you're in.

But then something shifts.

You're invited into a new meeting—different team, different priorities, different dynamics.

You speak the same way you always do.

But it doesn't land the same.

People don't know your track record. They don't have context for how you operate. Your usual level of contribution feels... neutral.

Not wrong.

Just not yet trusted.

That's when you realize something important:

Trust doesn't transfer automatically across environments.
It has to be re-established.

And that's where many leaders get frustrated.

They assume:
"I've already proven myself."

But trust at scale works differently.

What Strong Leaders Do

Strong leaders understand that **trust is contextual—and scalable only through consistency across environments**.

They don't assume credibility carries over.

They build it intentionally in each new space.

They focus on three things:

1. Establishing Clarity Quickly

In new environments, strong leaders don't rush to contribute immediately.

They first understand:

- What matters here?
- How decisions are made

- What success looks like
- Where friction exists

They ask better questions before offering better answers.

This signals:

- Respect
- Awareness
- Intentional engagement

2. Adapting Without Losing Consistency

Strong leaders adjust their approach—but not their standards.

They may:

- Change how they communicate
- Adjust timing
- Modify level of detail

But they remain consistent in:

- Clarity
- Responsibility
- Follow-through

That balance builds trust faster.

3. Reinforcing Reliability Across Teams

Trust at scale is built when people begin to say:

- "They're consistent—no matter where they are"

- "They operate the same way across teams"
- "You can rely on them"

Strong leaders understand:

Consistency across environments creates reputation.

And reputation allows your leadership to extend beyond direct interaction.

The Expansion Point

This is where leadership begins to move beyond:

- Individual contribution
- Single-team influence

Into:

- Cross-team trust
- Broader visibility
- Expanded responsibility

Not because of title.

Because of pattern.

The Common Mistake

At this stage, many leaders make a subtle error.

They try to **prove themselves quickly**.

They:

- Speak too early
- Push too hard
- Over-contribute before understanding context

This can create resistance.

Not because their input is wrong.

Because trust hasn't caught up yet.

Strong leaders resist that urge.

They build trust first.

Then scale contribution.

Apply This Now

This is where your leadership becomes portable.

1. Enter New Environments with Awareness

Before contributing, ask:

- What is the priority here?
- What matters most in this space?
- How is success measured?

Understanding increases effectiveness.

2. Contribute with Intent, Not Volume

In new settings:

- Say less—but make it count

- Focus on clarity
- Add value early, even if small

Precision builds trust faster than volume.

3. Maintain Your Leadership Standard

Regardless of environment:

- Stay clear
- Stay accountable
- Stay consistent

Adapt style—not substance.

4. Build Trust Through Follow-Through

After contributing:

- Reinforce decisions
- Support execution
- Stay engaged

Trust grows when people see consistency beyond the moment.

5. Think Beyond the Room

Ask:

"How does my behavior here shape how people experience me elsewhere?"

Because leadership at scale is built through:

- Patterns

- Reputation
- Reliability

When people begin to trust you in multiple environments, your leadership stops being situational.

It becomes transferable.

Chapter 10 Reflection

Notice → Interpret → Practice → Prepare

NOTICE
Where have you seen trust accelerate or slow down progress?

INTERPRET
What behaviors contributed to that pattern?

PRACTICE
Identify one area where you can increase consistency this week.

PREPARE
How does consistency expand your influence beyond your role?

CARRY FORWARD
Trust grows through what you repeat.

Trust extends your influence.

What you build in others determines how far it goes.

Chapter 11

Developing Others Early

Leadership expands the moment it is no longer about you.

Every leader eventually reaches a point where their impact is no longer defined by what they accomplish alone—but by what they build in others.

Every mentor was once coached. Every coach eventually becomes a mentor.

That transition does not begin when you are given authority. It begins the moment you realize someone is learning from how you show up—even informally.

This is where many leaders wait too long.

They assume development starts with position. That coaching requires authority. That mentorship is something you do once you are established.

But leadership does not wait for permission.

People are already learning from you.

They are watching how you respond under pressure.
How you handle frustration.
How you speak about others.
How you carry responsibility.

Development is already happening.

The question is whether it is intentional.

Developing others early does not require formal structure. It begins with small, deliberate actions:

- Sharing context instead of just direction.

- Explaining the "why," not just the "what."

- Creating space for others to think, not just execute.

- Offering feedback that builds, not just corrects.

These actions multiply.

They do more than improve performance—they build capability. They prepare others to operate with clarity, not just compliance.

Over time, this changes how you are experienced as a leader.

You are no longer just someone people rely on.

You are someone who makes others better.

And that is where leadership begins to extend beyond your direct reach.

In Practice

You're working closely with someone newer to the environment.

They're capable—but inconsistent.

Sometimes they perform well. Other times they miss details, hesitate, or need more direction than expected.

You notice it quickly.

Because you've been there.

You understand what they're trying to navigate:

- Unclear expectations
- New systems
- Pressure to perform without full context

At first, it's easier to just do it yourself.

You correct small things without explaining them. You step in to ensure quality. You move faster by carrying more.

The work gets done.

But something else happens.

They don't improve at the same pace.

And over time, you realize:

You've been solving the problem—but not developing the person.

That's the moment Chapter 11 is about.

What Strong Leaders Do

Strong leaders understand that **development doesn't start with authority**.

It starts with attention.

They don't wait until they have a title to begin developing others.

They start early—through how they:

- Explain
- Clarify

- Coach
- Create space for others to grow

They recognize:

If you only focus on output, you limit your impact.
If you develop people, you expand it.

The Shift from Doing to Developing

Most emerging leaders default to doing.

Because:

- It's faster
- It's more controlled
- It feels efficient

But development requires a different posture.

It requires:

- Slowing down
- Explaining thinking
- Allowing others to try—and sometimes struggle

Strong leaders shift from:

"I'll handle this"

To:

"Let me show you how to handle this"

And eventually:

"You take this—I'll support you"

That progression builds capability.

The Early Leadership Advantage

Developing others early creates an advantage many leaders overlook.

It builds:

- Trust
- Credibility
- Influence

Not because you have authority.

Because people experience you as someone who:

- Helps them improve
- Invests in their growth
- Makes them better

That reputation compounds.

What Development Looks Like in Practice

Development is not formal.

It's embedded in everyday interactions.

1. Explaining the "Why"

Instead of just giving direction:

"Do it this way"

Strong leaders add:

"Here's why this matters…"

This builds understanding—not just compliance.

2. Giving Specific Feedback

Not:
"Good job"
or
"That needs work"

But:

- "Here's what worked well…"
- "Here's what you can improve…"
- "Here's how to approach it next time…"

Clarity accelerates growth.

3. Creating Ownership

Instead of taking over:

- Ask them to lead a portion
- Let them present
- Let them decide within boundaries

Ownership builds confidence.

4. Allowing Space for Learning

This is where many leaders struggle.

Development requires allowing:

- Imperfection
- Adjustment
- Growth over time

Strong leaders don't expect immediate perfection.

They expect progression.

The Multiplication Principle

When you develop others, something shifts.

Your impact is no longer limited to:

- What you do
- What you say

It expands to:

- What others can do because of you

That's multiplication.

And it starts long before formal leadership roles.

The Common Mistake

Many leaders delay development because they believe:

"I need to be more experienced first"

But development is not about having all the answers.

It's about:

- Sharing what you know
- Being honest about what you don't
- Helping others think more clearly

You don't need perfection to develop people.

You need intention.

Apply This Now

You can begin developing others immediately.

1. Identify One Person You Can Support

Look around:

- A teammate
- A peer
- Someone newer

Start there.

2. Explain Your Thinking

Don't just act—explain:

- Why you made a decision
- How you approached a problem

- What you considered

This builds understanding.

3. Give One Piece of Useful Feedback

Keep it simple:

- One strength
- One improvement
- One suggestion

Consistency matters more than volume.

4. Create One Opportunity for Ownership

Let someone:

- Take the lead
- Present an idea
- Own a small piece of work

Then support them through it.

5. Decide What You Want to Multiply

This is the core question:

What do you want others to learn from you?

Because whether you're intentional or not:

You are already teaching something.

The moment you begin developing others, your leadership stops being defined by what you produce.

It becomes defined by what continues because of you.

Chapter 11 Reflection

Notice → Interpret → Practice → Prepare

NOTICE
Who is already learning from how you show up?

INTERPRET
What are they learning—intentionally or unintentionally?

PRACTICE
Invest in one person this week through clarity, feedback, or support.

PREPARE
How does developing others expand your leadership impact?

CARRY FORWARD
Leadership grows when others grow because of you.

When others grow because of you, leadership begins to multiply.

These are small—but they create *flow discipline*.

Chapter 12

Leadership That Multiplies

At its highest level, leadership is not measured by control.

It is measured by continuity.

What continues because of you?
What improves because you were there?
What remains strong after you step away?

This is the difference between leadership that performs and
leadership that multiplies.

Performing leaders deliver results.

Multiplying leaders build systems, people, and standards that
continue delivering results without them.

This is where everything in this book comes together.

Awareness ensures you do not repeat what weakens culture.
Posture ensures you carry responsibility instead of deflecting it.
Discipline ensures you remain teachable and avoid shortcuts.
Contribution ensures what you see becomes useful.
Development ensures others grow alongside you.

Multiplication is the result of all of it.

It is not something you start at the end.

It is something you build all the way through.

Multiplying leaders think differently.

They do not ask:
"How do I get this done?"

They ask:
"How do I build this so it continues?"

They do not measure success by personal output.

They measure it by collective capability.

They do not hold leadership tightly.

They extend it.

This is where stewardship becomes real.

You are no longer managing access, protecting position, or controlling outcomes.

You are building something that will outlast you.

That is the responsibility you carry forward.

In Practice

You look around and realize something has changed.

Not in your title.

In your impact.

People begin to approach you differently.

They ask for your input earlier.
They trust your perspective more quickly.
They begin to adopt how you think, how you communicate, how you approach problems.

You hear your language repeated.

Not exactly—but close enough to recognize.

Someone explains something the way you would have.
Someone asks a question you've asked before.
Someone handles a situation in a way that reflects how you've coached them.

And in that moment, you see it:

Your leadership is no longer contained to your actions.

It's showing up in others.

That's multiplication.

What Strong Leaders Do

Strong leaders don't just build capability.

They build **continuity**.

They understand that leadership is not measured only by:

- What gets done
- What improves
- What outcomes are achieved

But by:

What continues when they are not present.

They focus on three outcomes:

1. Leaders Who Think Independently

They don't create followers who wait.

They develop people who:

- Ask better questions
- Make informed decisions
- Operate with clarity

Because dependence limits growth.

Independence expands it.

2. Leaders Who Carry Standards

Strong leaders don't just model behavior.

They transfer it.

They ensure others understand:

- What good looks like
- What matters most
- What should not change

This creates consistency beyond the individual.

3. Leaders Who Develop Others

This is the multiplier.

They don't stop at developing one level.

They teach others to:

- Coach

- Clarify
- Invest in people

Because:

Leadership that multiplies does not stop with you.
It continues through others.

The Compounding Effect

Multiplication doesn't feel dramatic.

It feels gradual.

- One conversation
- One coached moment
- One shift in thinking

But over time, it compounds.

You begin to see:

- Fewer repeated problems
- Stronger independent decisions
- More consistent execution

Not because you're doing more.

Because others are.

The Legacy Question

At some point, every leader faces a question—whether they ask it
directly or not:

What remains because I was here?

Not:

- What did I accomplish?
- What did I control?

But:

- What improved?
- Who grew?
- What continues?

This is where leadership becomes legacy.

The Common Misunderstanding

Many leaders believe legacy is something that happens at the end.

It's not.

Legacy is built in:

- Daily interactions
- Small decisions
- Repeated behaviors

It's formed long before it's recognized.

Apply This Now

Multiplication is not a future concept.

It starts immediately.

1. Teach What You Know

Don't wait until you're an expert.

Share:

- How you think
- How you approach problems
- What you've learned

Teaching accelerates growth—for both people.

2. Reinforce Standards Consistently

Be clear about:

- What matters
- What good looks like
- What should improve

Consistency builds culture.

3. Develop Developers

Encourage others to:

- Give feedback
- Support teammates
- Share knowledge

This expands your impact beyond direct interaction.

4. Step Back Strategically

112

As others grow:

- Let them lead
- Let them decide
- Let them take ownership

Support—but don't control.

5. Define Your Leadership Intentionally

Ask yourself:

What do I want to continue—even when I'm not here?

Because that answer shapes how you lead today.

Bringing It Together

This book has followed a progression:

- You learned to **see clearly** (Awareness)
- You learned to **choose your response** (Posture)
- You learned to **make your perspective useful** (Contribution)
- And now, you understand how to **extend your impact through others** (Multiplication)

This is the full arc of leadership.

Not defined by title.

Leadership that multiplies is not measured by what you build alone.

It is measured by what continues—and grows—because of you.

Chapter 12 Reflection

Notice → Interpret → Practice → Prepare

NOTICE

Where have you seen leadership that continued beyond the individual?

INTERPRET

What made that possible?

PRACTICE

Take one step this week to build something that continues without you.

PREPARE

How does multiplication redefine success in leadership?

CARRY FORWARD

Leadership that lasts is leadership that multiplies.

Part III Closing Reflection – From Contribution to Multiplication

From Perspective to Responsibility

At this point, your leadership should feel different.

Not because your role has changed.

Because your impact has.

You've moved from:

- noticing problems
- to choosing your response
- to making your perspective useful

And now, something more subtle is happening.

People are beginning to rely on you.

Not just for answers—but for clarity.

Not just for input—but for direction.

Not just for performance—but for how you shape the environment.

This is where leadership expands.

Because once your presence consistently improves outcomes, expectations change.

You are no longer evaluated only on what you do.

You are evaluated on what happens around you.

And that is where multiplication begins.

The question is no longer whether you can contribute.
It is whether others are stronger because you were there.

NOTICE

Where have you already begun to influence others—intentionally or unintentionally?

INTERPRET

What patterns are you reinforcing through how you show up each day?

PRACTICE

Identify one behavior you will model consistently moving forward.

PREPARE

Who will be better because of how you lead from this point on?

CARRY FORWARD

Write one commitment you will not negotiate with yourself:

Leadership is no longer something you are preparing for.

It is something you are responsible for.

You started this book trying to understand leadership.
Now you are responsible for how it continues.

Epilogue

A Letter From the Leader You Are Becoming

If you've made it this far, I hope you can feel it: you've already been practicing the posture this book keeps returning to—more than you may realize.

Leadership is not something you arrive at.

It is something you carry—forward, daily, and often without recognition.

When you began this book, you were asked to notice.

To pay attention to language, behavior, and the quiet signals that shape leadership long before titles are involved.

Now, you are no longer just noticing.

You are deciding.

Deciding how you will respond when leadership is unclear.
Deciding what you will carry forward—and what you will leave behind.
Deciding what others will learn from you, whether you intend to teach it or not.

Because they will.

The way you speak.
The way you handle pressure.
The way you treat people when it would be easier not to.

All of it is being observed.

All of it is being learned.

And over time, it will be repeated.

That is the responsibility of leadership.

Not just to perform well.

But to ensure that what comes after you is stronger than what came before you.

You were never meant to fix this generation.

You were meant to become the leader the next one deserves.

And now, that work belongs to you.

You've seen how leadership is built in the small stuff—trust, consistency, and what it feels like to be on the receiving end of your decisions when the path isn't clear. And you've seen where it ends up if no one interrupts it: sooner or later, every leader becomes *"they"*—the unnamed reference people reach for when explaining how things are done, or why they aren't.

You're already influencing people. What matters is what your influence is growing in them: more confidence and capability— or more hesitation and distance.

Soon enough, someone younger will try your patience. They'll ask questions that feel premature. They'll push on a rule you've stopped noticing. And you'll feel the old pull—to explain away a person by blaming a generation, to trade coaching for a label because it's faster and safer. When you feel that pull, you're not alone—and you still get to choose what you do next.

When that happens, give yourself a beat—and be kind to yourself in it. Pausing is part of leading.

Remember what it felt like to be treated like a problem before anyone bothered to see your potential. Remember the difference it made when someone explained the *why*, not just the task. And remember the leaders who built confidence in you without making you dependent on them.

Leadership isn't demonstrated by becoming irreplaceable. It shows up when the work holds up—and people keep growing—because you were intentional about what you built and what you handed off. And that starts long before a title makes it official.

You won't lead perfectly. You'll misread a situation. You'll get tired. And some days, control will feel cleaner than coaching. What matters isn't flawlessness—it's whether you return to the posture you chose early: to steward instead of dominate, to prepare instead of preserve.

The people who come after you won't need a flawless leader. They'll need someone present—someone who tells the truth, sets standards, and stays invested in their growth. They'll also need you to remember that leadership is temporary even when its impact isn't.

Someday, people will talk about your leadership when you're not in the room.

It won't sound like your intentions, and it probably won't start with your title.

What they'll remember is what it felt like to be around you: developed or dismissed, informed or managed, invited into responsibility—or kept at arm's length.

That story gets written in ordinary days—meetings, deadlines, hallway conversations, the way you talk when you're tired, and the way you talk when you're frustrated.

So lead with intention—especially in the quiet moments. Those are often the ones people remember most, and they're the ones you can choose again tomorrow.

You are no longer just becoming.

You are now responsible for what comes next.

Someone will learn leadership by watching you—whether you intend it or not.

The question is no longer what kind of leaders you experienced.

One day, someone will point to a moment like this—
and realize they learned leadership by watching you.

Leadership Carry Forward

Before you close this book, write one commitment you will carry forward:

- What will you do differently starting now?
- Who will you develop intentionally?
- What will your leadership be known for—when you are not in the room?

Leadership is not what you finish here.

It is what you repeat next.

Reflection Worksheet

The Leader You Are Choosing to Become

This page isn't meant to be rushed.
Come back to it—especially as your responsibility grows.

1. Awareness

What leadership behaviors or language stood out to you while reading this book?
(Consider moments that made you uncomfortable, reflective, or newly aware.)

2. Inherited Patterns

What leadership habits or assumptions have you absorbed without questioning?
(From mentors, supervisors, organizational culture, or "the way things are done.")

3. Perspective as Strength

What do you see or experience that others above you may not?
(Consider technology, workflows, culture, communication, or emerging risks.)

How can you translate this perspective into contribution rather than complaint?

4. Early Multiplication

Who already looks to you—formally or informally—for guidance, clarity, or example?

What is one thing you can begin teaching or modeling now—before you are asked?

5. Leadership Posture

When frustration arises, which direction do you tend to lean?

☐ Blame
☐ Withdrawal
☐ Control
☐ Responsibility
☐ Coaching

What posture do you want to practice deliberately going forward?

6. Replacement Mindset

If you stepped away tomorrow, what knowledge, habits, or standards would disappear with you?

What is one step you can take to make your role less dependent on you personally?

7. Commitment

Finish this sentence honestly:

As a leader—now and in the future—I commit to becoming someone who...

8. Revisit Point

Pick a date to return, reread what you wrote, and see what's changed:

Date: _____

Leadership is not revealed in moments of power.
It is formed in moments of intention.

124

ABOUT THE AUTHOR

Thomas Wigington is a senior leader with more than 25 years of experience leading large, complex organizations where clarity, accountability, and disciplined execution determine outcomes. He has led geographically distributed teams, supported mission-critical operations, and advised senior leaders on strategy, risk, and organizational performance.

His leadership approach is grounded in a simple belief: leadership is not defined by authority—it is revealed through responsibility, consistency, and how people are developed over time. Throughout his career, he has focused on building systems that scale, developing leaders at every level, and creating environments where trust and performance reinforce one another.

Drawing from extensive experience in high-stakes, highly regulated environments, Wigington brings a practical, structured perspective to leadership—one that prioritizes clarity over complexity and action over theory. His work centers on helping emerging and experienced leaders alike build credibility early, lead with intention, and create impact that extends beyond their immediate role.

Stewards Not Gatekeepers reflects his commitment to developing leaders who do more than perform well—they build people, shape culture, and leave systems stronger than they found them.

He writes to help leaders build what lasts—through people, not position.

This is the first book released under QTR Foundry—where intentional leaders are forged—and published through The Foundry Press.